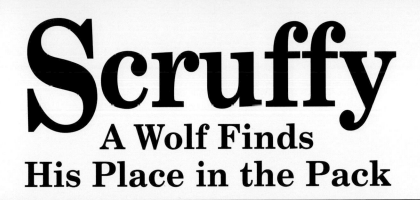

Scruffy
A Wolf Finds
His Place in the Pack

Jim Brandenburg
Edited by JoAnn Bren Guernsey

Walker and Company
New York

Scruffy finds a comfortable spot for a nap on the soft tundra.

Scruffy, a young white Arctic wolf, lives in a faraway frozen place called Ellesmere Island. He was born the year before I arrived, so he was no longer a pup. But he wasn't an adult member of his pack yet. If Scruffy had been human, he probably would have been called a teenager. He had a lot of the same problems people have trying to grow up. But he also had a bigger problem—staying alive.

The pack's home is covered with snow for most of the year.

Ellesmere Island is not far from the North Pole, so it is very cold—down to 70 degrees below zero in the winter. As if the cold isn't enough, Ellesmere also has fierce, biting winds, and it's as dry as a desert. The earth is frozen solid 1,000 feet below the surface. In the den where Scruffy and all the other pups were born, the back walls are covered with ice. There are snow fields that never melt, even during the summer. And icebergs loom nearby like white, watchful giants.

Playing king of the hill, Scruffy and a pack member climb to the top of an iceberg.

Trailing the Arctic wolf pack at 50 degrees below zero.

 arrived on Ellesmere Island during a cold, wintry spring, and I stayed through the summer. *National Geographic* magazine had sent me there to photograph all the Arctic animals. But my eyes and camera kept turning toward the wolves. Especially Scruffy.

A wolf pack is very much like a human family. In fact, many scientists believe that no other animal "family" acts more like humans than a wolf pack.

Life can be difficult for the Arctic wolf pack in the winter.

Scruffy awakes from a long nap.

Wolves mate for life, and the pack is usually made up of brothers, sisters, aunts, and uncles. Together, this family shares the duties of hunting, watching for danger, and raising the young.

Most young wolves strike out on their own after a year to find mates and form their own packs. It's a mystery why Scruffy stayed with this pack instead of leaving his parents. He may have been the strongest pup and driven off the others. Or he may have been the weakest one, who was not seen as a threat. Whatever the reason, he stayed and was protected by the pack.

Scruffy's father, the leader of the pack, is always in charge.

ince my camp was near the wolf den, it wasn't long before I got to know the members of this family of wolves. Slight differences in the way each of them looked and acted helped me to tell them apart better each day. Some appeared to be stronger and bolder than the others. These *dominant* wolves were better hunters and seemed to be the most important members of the pack.

Scruffy was not one of the dominant wolves. He was timid and depended on the others to take care of him. And he was by far the messiest of the pack—that's how he got his name.

Scruffy always seemed to have huge clumps of fur hanging from him.

The leaders of the pack always eat first.

he leader of a wolf pack is called the alpha male (or in some cases, the alpha female). On Ellesmere Island, the pack was led by a strong alpha pair. They were always the first to attack during a hunt and the first to eat after a kill. Until these two ate as much as they wanted, none of the other wolves could get even a scrap of food.

Scruffy was the lowest-ranking member of his pack. He ate last and had to beg for food. I watched him trying to get approval and affection from his "superiors," but they usually beat him up instead.

The more dominant wolves stood tall and moved with confidence. Their beautiful white coats bristled and their tails and ears pointed upward. Scruffy and the other low-ranking wolves moved in a way that said, *please don't hurt me.* They kept their bodies low to the ground, slinking and cowering. When the dominant pack members were around, Scruffy's ears flattened and his tail curled between his legs. If he got beat up, he'd soon come back for more, as though *this* time things would be better.

Dominant wolves move with confidence.

But as badly as the grown-ups appeared to treat him, Scruffy seemed very lonely when the rest of the pack had gone on a hunt. He sat and howled, watching the horizon for their return.

Left behind, Scruffy sounds out his loneliness.

 cruffy had a goofy way about him. He was more careless than the rest of the wolves and didn't seem to have the common sense he needed. So he usually messed up when he tried to do adult tasks. He rarely went on hunts with the pack, and the few times he did, he seemed too unsure of himself to be a good hunter.

In a careless moment, Scruffy gets charged by a musk ox.

A foolish Scruffy gets dive-bombed while looking for eggs to eat.

One day, Scruffy wanted to eat the eggs from the nest of some Arctic birds called long-tailed jaegers. Adult wolves help themselves to these eggs without much trouble. But Scruffy couldn't seem to figure out how to do it. Over and over, the jaegers dive-bombed him and knocked his head with their feet. He finally gave up, with his tail between his legs and a silly, confused look on his face.

The pups are content when the den is guarded by Scruffy.

ut there was one thing Scruffy could do well. And it soon became clear that his role in the pack was very important. In July, six gray balls of fur stumbled out of the den and waddled around on oversized paws. The pups may have been big and sturdy enough to face the world outside the den, but they needed a lot of help. And Scruffy was the pups' main baby-sitter.

Two pups playfully fight for possession of a stick.

The pups always trusted Scruffy to lead them on adventures.

I was surprised by the change in Scruffy once the pups entered the picture. When the adults left on a hunt, the baby-sitter was in charge. Suddenly Scruffy became a cocky, dominant wolf. He stood and walked much taller, his tail and ears perked up. With the pups, he seemed to say, *Aha. I'm in charge now. You pups better obey or I'll beat you up.*

Scruffy played with the pups and took them on walks. He howled with them and wrestled. He even played tug-of-war with them using a piece of fur. Scruffy would sit there for a while, gently tugging and letting a pup feel powerful. Then he'd suddenly yank it back hard, forcing the pup to grow stronger and more alert.

Scruffy taught the pups to be strong with games of tug-of-war.

Scruffy was an expert bully when the pack was away hunting.

But Scruffy's job was not merely to play. It is a sad fact that at least half of the young wolves in this harsh climate die. So the most important task of any wolf in charge of the pups is to toughen them up, even if the methods seem terribly cruel. Scruffy turned out to be an expert bully. He growled and nipped at the pups, tackled and shook them until they yelped in pain. At last, Scruffy could be the "superior" one. Of course, he had to keep an eye open for the return of the pack. If he got caught acting and looking dominant, he could get punished.

Scruffy loved to make the pups beg for attention.

How did the pups feel about their baby-sitter? He seemed to be their hero. They watched his every move as though he were the best wolf who ever lived. While resting quietly, they sat at his feet and raised their small snouts toward his. And they obeyed him . . . most of the time.

The pups stand at attention while Scruffy trots by for inspection.

Scruffy, the hero of the pups, sometimes felt like a king.

The alpha female brings an Arctic fox to the pups for a hunting lesson.

cruffy often helped the adult wolves teach the pups lessons in the art of becoming a wolf. One time, the alpha female brought an Arctic fox back to the den to give to the pups. Scruffy urged the pups to "kill" the already dead fox over and over again. In each round of this tiring game, one pup would growl, grab the fox by the throat, and shake it. The most dominant pup would eventually steal the tattered "prize" and run around and around, chased by the others.

Life for Arctic wolves is a daily life-and-death struggle. Death by disease, injury, or starvation is always a threat. This is why the ranking system in a wolf pack is important. For those who do not work and fit together well with the others, there is no room and not enough food. In spite of all his apparent faults, Scruffy's skill as a baby-sitter made him valuable to the pack.

Scruffy urges the pups to "kill" the already dead fox.

The pups during their first Arctic snow.

By August, the first snows began to fall, and I had to pack up and leave. The pups had grown a lot, and their fur, which had been gray, was now turning white like the adults' coats—for camouflage in the snow. But they still had so much to learn. I felt tremendous sadness the morning I left. How many of these pups would live? I wondered. Then I looked at Scruffy. Would he survive another winter?

Scruffy and the pups play on an iceberg.

I returned the following May to film the pack for a *National Geographic* television show. I found the pack had changed in surprising ways. Another male had taken over as leader. The calm, gentle female who had been the pups' mother the year before was now the alpha female. I still thought of her as "Mom."

The gentle face of Mom.

Scruffy's rank in the pack hadn't changed. And neither had his role as baby-sitter. He was hovering by Mom and seemed eager to begin caring for her new litter. When he poked his head inside the den, he was greeted with a chorus of puppy growls.

The newborn pups groan and growl as they snuggle against each other with their soft fur.

The pups huddle to stay warm deep inside the frost-covered den.

om was as good-natured as before. She even let me go into the den one day to take photographs of the tiny pups. I wriggled down the narrow passageway into a cool and damp room. It smelled sweetly of puppy fur. In the beam of my flashlight I saw the four pups, shivering and clinging to each other. One of them pointed its muzzle at me and growled. At three weeks old, it was already showing signs of dominance. Maybe it would be an alpha someday. I wondered if there might be another Scruffy in that litter too.

As soon as I came out of the den, Mom disappeared inside to make sure everything was all right. Scruffy stayed by the entrance and kept a watchful eye on me. He looked ready to take on this new litter. He'd teach them a thing or two.

Scruffy keeps a watchful eye on the den entrance.

**W**hen I finally had to leave several days later, Scruffy trotted along with me the whole way to the airstrip. After three miles, he stopped and perked up his ears. His body pointed to a nearby herd of caribou, and he made a charge. The caribou had little trouble getting away from him, and Scruffy was soon lying on the ground, scratching. But he looked at me, in that goofy way of his, as if to say, *What do you think of me now?*

Scruffy was continually looking for approval, even from me.

*To Dr. Arthur C. Aufderheide—who, when I was a scruffy young pup,
brought me to the Arctic and showed me the way.*

First published in the United States of America in 1996 by Walker Publishing Company, Inc.

Published simultaneously in Canada by Thomas Allen & Son Canada,
Limited, Markham, Ontario

Library of Congress Cataloging-in-Publication Data
Brandenburg, Jim
Scruffy: a wolf finds his place in the pack/Jim Brandenburg; edited by JoAnn Bren Guernsey.
p. cm.
Summary: A professional photographer visits Ellesmere Island near the North Pole and observes the behavior of a pack
of Arctic wolves, focusing on a timid male that becomes the pack's babysitter.
ISBN 0-8027-8445-3 (hardcover). —ISBN 0-8027-8446-1 (reinforced binding)
1. Wolves—Behavior—Northwest Territories—Ellesmere Island—Juvenile literature. 2. Wolves—Northwest Territories—
Ellesmere Island—Pictorial works—Juvenile literature. [1. Wolves—Habits and behavior. 2. Zoology—Arctic regions.]
I. Guernsey, JoAnn Bren II. Title.

QL737.C22B6355 1996
599.74'442—dc20

96-5446
CIP
AC

Photographs on pages 10 and 13 copyright © *National Geographic*

Printed in Hong Kong
2 4 6 8 10 9 7 5 3 1